CARIBBEAN CARNIVAL

Songs of the West Indies

IRVING BURGIE · Pictures by FRANÉ LESSAC

AFTERWORD BY ROSA GUY

TAMBOURINE BOOKS

NEW YORK

For Joanie
I.B.

For Ryan, Daniel, Luke, and Cody
F. L.

Compilation copyright © 1992 by Cherry Lane Music Publishing Company, Inc.
Afterword copyright © 1992 by Rosa Guy and Tambourine Books
Illustrations copyright © 1992 by Frané Lessac

DAY-O Music and lyrics by Irving Burgie and William Attaway. Copyright 1955, Renewed 1983 by Cherry Lane Music Publishing Company, Inc./Lord Burgess Music Publishing Company. (ASCAP)

MICHAEL ROW THE BOAT Traditional, arranged by Irving Burgie. Copyright 1992 by Cherry Lane Music Publishing Company, Inc./Lord Burgess Music Publishing Company. (ASCAP)

YELLOW BIRD (Choucounne) Traditional, arranged by Irving Burgie. Copyright 1955, Renewed 1983 by Irving Burgie. (ASCAP)

PANAMA TOMBÉ Traditional, arranged by Irving Burgie. Copyright 1992 by Cherry Lane Music Publishing Company, Inc./Lord Burgess Music Publishing Company. (ASCAP)

CHI CHI BUD Traditional, arranged by Irving Burgie. Copyright 1992 by Cherry Lane Music Publishing Company, Inc./Lord Burgess Music Publishing Company. (ASCAP)

MISSY LOST THE GOLD RING Traditional, arranged by Irving Burgie. Copyright 1992 by Cherry Lane Music Publishing Company, Inc./Lord Burgess Music Publishing Company. (ASCAP)

¡QUÉ BONITA BANDERA! Traditional, arranged by Irving Burgie. Copyright 1992 by Cherry Lane Music Publishing Company, Inc./Lord Burgess Music Publishing Company. (ASCAP)

KINGSTON MARKET Music and lyrics by Irving Burgie. Copyright 1961, Renewed 1989 by Cherry Lane Music Publishing Company, Inc./Lord Burgess Music Publishing Company. (ASCAP)

LITTLE GIRL IN THE RING Traditional, arranged by Irving Burgie. Copyright 1992 by Cherry Lane Music Publishing Company, Inc./Lord Burgess Music Publishing Company. (ASCAP)

I CARRY MY ACKEE Traditional, arranged by Irving Burgie. Copyright 1992 by Cherry Lane Music Publishing Company, Inc./Lord Burgess Music Publishing Company. (ASCAP)

JUDY DROWNED-ED Music and lyrics by Irving Burgie. Copyright 1957, Renewed 1985 by Cherry Lane Music Publishing Company, Inc./Lord Burgess Music Publishing Company. (ASCAP)

CAROLINA KARO Traditional, arranged by Irving Burgie. Copyright 1992 by Cherry Lane Music Publishing Company, Inc./Lord Burgess Music Publishing Company. (ASCAP)

JAMAICA FAREWELL Music and lyrics by Irving Burgie. Copyright 1955, Renewed 1983 by Cherry Lane Music Publishing Company, Inc./Lord Burgess Music Publishing Company. (ASCAP)

Library of Congress Cataloging in Publication Data

Caribbean carnival : songs of the West Indies /[compiled by]
Irving Burgie; illustrated by Frané Lessac.
p. of music. Calypso songs arr. for children. Includes chord symbols.
Summary: A collection of calypso, a uniquely West Indian
musical expression.
1. Calypso (Music)—West Indies. 2. Children's songs—West
Indies. [1. Calypso (Music) 2. West Indies—Songs and music.
3. Songs.] I. Burgie, Irving. II. Lessac, Frané, i11.
M1681.A1C37 1992 91-760838 CIP M AC
ISBN 0-688-10779-6 (trade). — ISBN 0-688-10780-X (lib.)

All rights reserved. No part of this book may be reproduced or
utilized in any form or by any means, electronic or mechanical,
including photocopying, recording, or by any information storage
or retrieval system, without permission in writing from the
Publisher. Inquiries should be addressed to Tambourine Books,
a division of William Morrow & Company, Inc.,
1350 Avenue of the Americas, New York, New York 10019.
Printed in the United States of America

The full-color illustrations were painted in gouache on paper.

1 3 5 7 9 10 8 6 4 2
FIRST EDITION

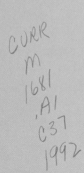

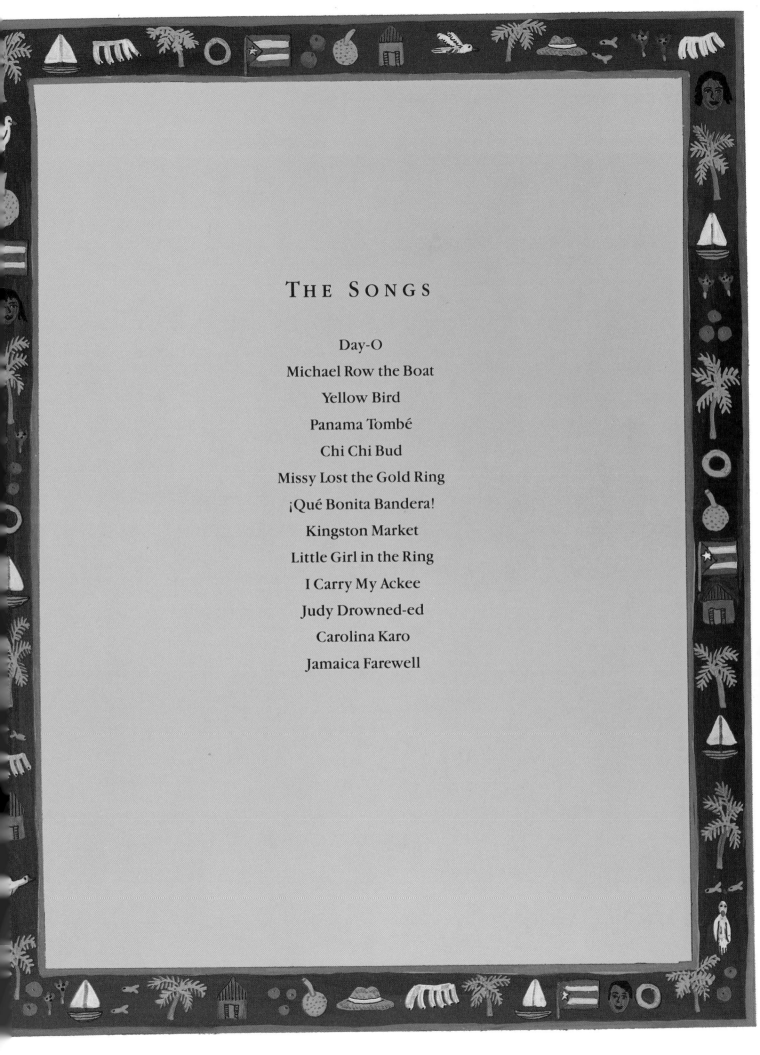

THE SONGS

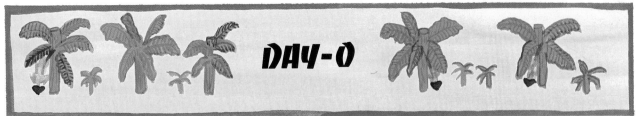

DAY-O

Moderately fast

Vocal solo

Day - o, day - o,— Day-light come— and me

wan' go home.— Day, me say day, me say day, me say day, me say day, me say

Fine

day - o. Day-light come— and me wan' go home.—

D

Work all night— on a drink of rum.— Day-light come— and me

A7   D

wan' go home. Stack ba - na - na till de morn - in' come.—

A7   D

Day-light come— and me wan' go home. Come, Mis - ter tal - ly man,

Day-light come___ and me wan' go home.
Day-light come___ and me wan' go home.

Six- hand, sev-en-hand,
Hide the dead-ly

eight-hand bunch.
black ta-ran-t'la.

Day-light come___ and me wan' go home.
Day-light come___ and me

1. wan' go home.

2. wan' go home.

D.C. al Fine

MICHAEL ROW THE BOAT

Moderately

Mi - chael, row the boat a - shore, hal - le - lu -

jah! Mi - chael, row the boat a - shore, hal - le - lu -

jah! 1. The wa-ter's deep and the wa-ter's wide, hal - le - lu -

jah! Row this boat to the oth - er side, hal - le - lu - jah!

Additional Lyrics

2. Tide is high and the boat is full, hallelujah!
   Everybody got to give a pull, hallelujah!

3. Brother, help me trim the sail, hallelujah!
   Gotta brace for another gale, hallelujah!

4. The spray is high but the keel is strong, hallelujah!
   Everybody come help along, hallelujah!

YELLOW BIRD

Moderate island beat

My friend has a yel - low bird that goes with him___ for a
But e - ven more than that, that it al - so knows___ how to

1.
walk.

2.
talk.

Yel - low bird, fly
Yel - low bird, come

up in co - co - nut tree;
back and an - swer for me.

I would like___ to know

how do flow - ers grow. Can you tell___ me when sum - mer comes___ a - gain?

How do riv - ers flow, what makes breez - es blow? Please an - swer for me.

PANAMA TOMBÉ

Moderately fast

Mwan sor - ti la vil Jae - mel, Pra - ley la Val -

lay Ar - ri - vay car - fou Be - nay,

Pan - a - ma tom - bay. Pan - a - ma tom - bay,

pan - a - ma tom - bay. Pan - a - ma tom - bay,

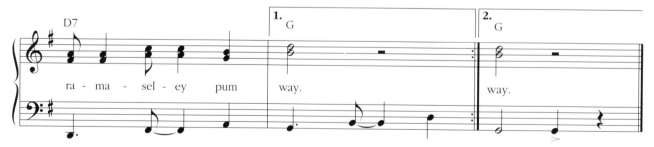

ra - ma - sel - ey pum way. way.

Translation

I left the village of Jacmel, passing through Vallee. As I arrived at
the crossroad of Bené, my panama hat fell off. If you come by,
retrieve it for me.

CHI CHI BUD

Moderately fast

(cry!) Chi chi bud, o! Some o' dem a hol - ler, some a cry! Chi chi bud, o!

Some o' dem a hol - ler, some a cry! Some a John Crow, some o' dem a hol - ler, some a

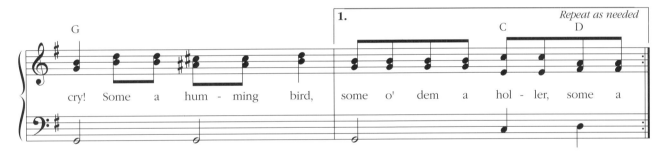

cry! Some a hum - ming bird, some o' dem a hol - ler, some a

Repeat as needed

some o' dem a hol - ler, some a cry!

Additional Lyrics

Some a sparrow,
Some a yellow bird,
Chi chi bud, o!
All a cry, o!
Some a pecker bird,
Some a blue bird,
Some a hawk bird,

Some a red bird,
Chi chi bud, o!
Chi chi bud, o!
Some a long leg,
Some a web foot,
Some a silver wing,
Some a coo coo bird,

Chi chi bud, o!
All a cry, o!
Lark
Some a bat wing,
Some a red breast,
Some a purple head,
Chi chi bud, o!

MISSY LOST THE GOLD RING

Moderately fast

Mis - sy lost,___ Mis - sy lost,___ Mis - sy lost___ the gol'

ring, O find 'em, find 'em, find 'em, find 'em, find 'em, lem - me

see.

Ring is lost,___ ring is lost,___
Woe is me,___ woe is me,___

lem - me here___ the sto - ry; O, find 'em, find 'em,
ring is lost___ al - read - y; O, find 'em, find 'em,

find 'em, find 'em, find 'em, lem - me see.
find 'em, find 'em, find 'em, lem - me

1.

see.

2.

see.

¡QUÉ BONITA BANDERA!

Moderately fast

Que bo-ni - ta ban - de - ra!   Que bo-ni - ta ban - de - ra!

Que bo-ni - ta ban - de - ra, la ban - de - ra Puer - to - ri - que-na!

Fine

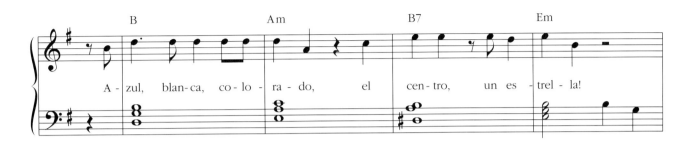

D.C. al Fine

Translation
What a beautiful flag! What a beautiful flag! What a beautiful flag,
the flag of Puerto Rico! Blue, white, red, in the center a star. What
a beautiful flag, the flag of Puerto Rico!

KINGSTON MARKET

Moderately fast

1. Have you ev - er seen a rain - bow or a gar - den bloom - ing bright? Heard the shuf - fle of a thou - sand feet or drums from morn - ing till night?

Chorus

Come we go down, come we go down, come we go down to King - ston Mar - ket. Come we go down, come we go down, down to King - ston Mar - ket.

Additional Lyrics

2. Buy your tamarind and soursop,
   Mangoes and cassava,
   Breadfruit, okra, salad greens,
   Tangerines and guava. *(To Chorus)*

LITTLE GIRL IN THE RING

Moderately fast

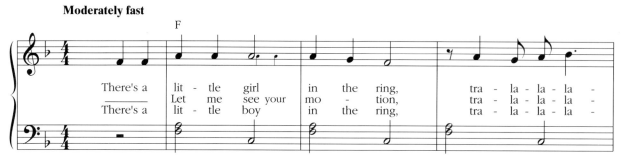

There's a lit - tle girl in the ring, tra - la - la - la - la -
Let me see your mo - tion, tra - la - la - la -
There's a lit - tle boy in the ring, tra - la - la - la -

la; There's a lit - tle girl in the ring, tra - la -
la; Let me see your mo - tion, tra - la -
la; There's a lit - tle boy in the ring, tra - la -

F

la - la - la. Lit - tle girl in the ring, tra - la - la - la - la;
la - la - la. Let me see your mo - tion, tra - la - la - la - la;
la - la - la. Lit - tle boy in the ring, tra - la - la - la - la;

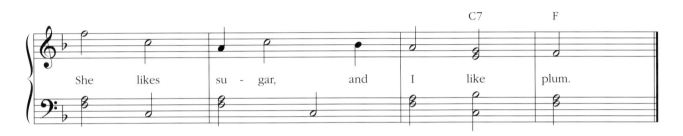

C7   F

She likes su - gar, and I like plum.

I CARRY MY ACKEE

Moderately fast

I car-ry my ack — ee to Lin-stead Mar — ket, not a pen — ny worth
Ev — 'ry-bod — y come look them, look them, not a pen — ny worth
Ev — 'ry-bod — y come feel them, feel them, not a pen — ny worth

sell. I car-ry my ack — ee to Lin-stead Mar — ket,
sell. Ev — 'ry-bod — y come look them, look them,
sell. Ev — 'ry-bod — y come feel them, feel them,

not a pen — ny worth sell. Oh, what a night, what a night!
not a pen — ny worth sell.
not a pen — ny worth sell.

What a Sat — ur-day night! Oh, what a

night, what a night! What a Sat-ur-day night! night!

JUDY DROWNED-ED

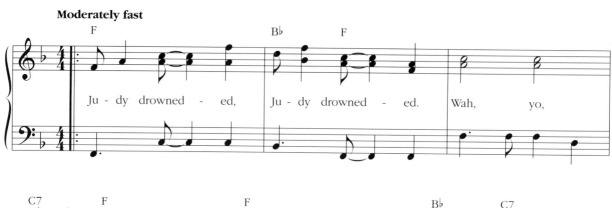

Moderately fast

F   B♭   F

Ju - dy drowned - ed,   Ju - dy drowned - ed.   Wah,   yo,

C7   F   F   B♭   C7

Ju - dy drowned - ed!

Ju - dy's ma - ma sent   her to mar - ket.
Ju - dy was walk - ing   'cross the wa - ter.
Went up to Ju - dy's   moth - er's shed.____

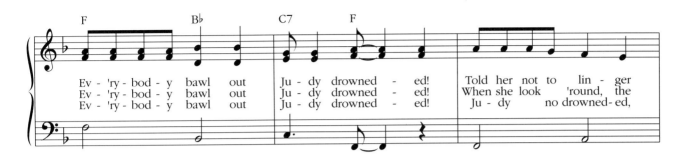

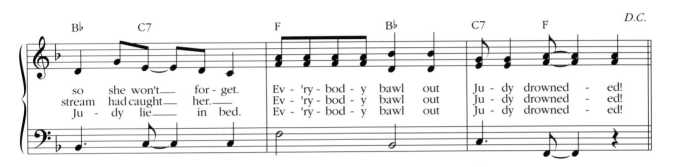

Ev-'ry-bod-y bawl out | Ju-dy drowned — ed! | Told her not to lin-ger
Ev-'ry-bod-y bawl out | Ju-dy drowned — ed! | When she look 'round, the
Ev-'ry-bod-y bawl out | Ju-dy drowned — ed! | Ju-dy no drowned-ed,

D.C.

so she won't — for-get. | Ev-'ry-bod-y bawl out | Ju-dy drowned — ed!
stream had caught — her. — | Ev-'ry-bod-y bawl out | Ju-dy drowned — ed!
Ju-dy lie — in bed. | Ev-'ry-bod-y bawl out | Ju-dy drowned — ed!

CAROLINA KARO

Translation

Carolina Karo,
Dance the congo until you are tired,
Until the ears are ringing.

JAMAICA FAREWELL

Bright island beat

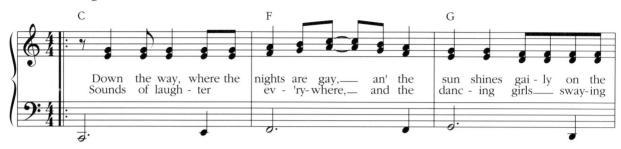

Down the way, where the nights are gay,— an' the sun shines gai - ly on the
Sounds of laugh - ter ev - 'ry-where,— and the danc - ing girls— sway-ing

moun - tain top,— I took a trip on a sail - ing ship,— an' when I
to and fro.— I must de - clare my heart is there,— tho' I've

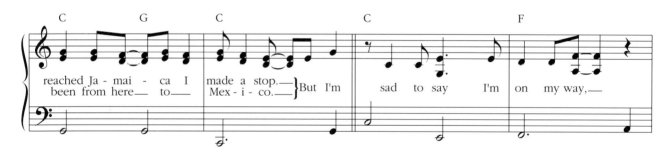

reached Ja - mai - ca I made a stop.— But I'm sad to say I'm on my way,—
been from here to— Mex - i - co.—

won't be back for man - y a day.— My heart is down,— my head is turn-ing a-round;— I had to

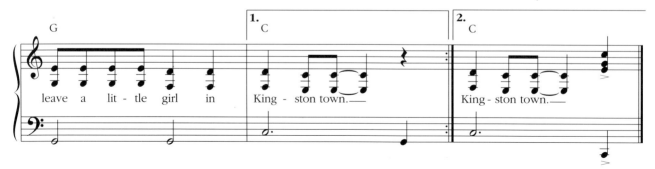

1. leave a lit - tle girl in King - ston town.—

2. King - ston town.—

ABOUT THE SONGS

Calypso can be traced directly to Africa. The African *griot* recorded tales through song—tales of little significance, tales of tragedies. Sung by young and old, gaining in lyricism through the years, and interwoven into the fabric of the people's culture, the tradition of storytelling was first brought to the Western Hemisphere by the enslaved people of African nations during the sixteenth century. On the islands of the Caribbean and along the coasts of South America, the tradition flourished in the cane fields and coffee plantations, changing in language as warring European nations won or lost their possessions.

With emancipation many freed slaves from smaller islands flooded into Trinidad, the wealthy island where land was promised to freed men who wanted to cultivate it. The joy of being free, of owning land, brought new vitality to their songs. Legend has it that in Trinidad, where freed men of all languages converged and new words were created on the demand of the moment, a man coined the name calypso while singing to his lady, "I call you with mi lip press so." A more widely accepted theory traces the term to *kaiso,* a West African cheer of approval that is still commonly shouted during the annual calypso carnival in Trinidad.

Calypso songs are rich in humor—chatty, gossipy, catchy, and political. Slowly they crept into the cultural beat of the English speaking islands and were brought to the United States in the migration of the early twentieth century.

Many Caribbean songs deal with the everyday work of the islanders. Irving Burgie's *Day-O* is inspired by the chants of Jamaican laborers loading banana boats. *Michael Row the Boat,* adopted as a spiritual in the American South and beyond, originated on the fishing boats of the Bahamas. *Kingston Market* and *I Carry My Ackee,* both set in Jamaica, are two of the many ballads drawn from the lively markets of the West Indies. (The tropical fruit of the akee tree is a favorite island dish when cooked with salt fish and rice.)

Other songs are all about play. *Little Girl in the Ring* is a Caribbean ring-around-the-rosy, while *Missy Lost the Gold Ring* is a children's game from Guyana, a republic on the Caribbean coast of South America with strong cultural links to the West Indies. *¡Qué Bonita Bandera!* invites children to parade with the red, white, and blue flag of Puerto Rico.

Calypso songs often sprang from topical commentary on long forgotten events. *Judy Drowned-ed* preserves the story of a Jamaican girl washed away by a river and reported dead by her neighbors before being rescued downstream. *Panama Tombé,* which involves not Panama but a panama hat, is believed to be rooted in satiric commentary on a pompous Haitian official. (The French-Creole words have been rendered phonetically here and for *Carolina Karo,* which moves to the beat of the Congo, a drum-pounding Haitian folk dance based on African ritual.)

And many Caribbean songs celebrate nature, including *Chi Chi Bud,* which evokes the birds of Jamaica in a raucous chorus of voices, and the gentle *Yellow Bird,* originally a Creole song from Haiti, with versions now sung on all the islands of the West Indies.

Setting and story, work and play, come together in ballads like Irving Burgie's *Jamaica Farewell.* Mr. Burgie, by far the most widely known lyricist and composer of Caribbean songs, has selected the songs in this book for young and old alike to sing and enjoy together.

—ROSA GUY